# SELF HELP HUNGER PROGRAM
## *The Original Herstory*
### VOL. 1

**By Aunti Frances Moore**

Edited by Maya Ram

A POOR Press Publication

ISBN 978-1-956534-13-9

Thank you to POOR Press team for design and copy-editing.
Edited by Maya Ram
Cover and interior design by A.S. Ikeda

**A POOR Press Publication © 2024 Frances Moore. All Rights Reserved.**
POOR Press is a poor and indigenous people-led press dedicated to publishing the books and scholarship of youth, adults, and elders in poverty locally and globally.

**www.poormagazine.org**
**www.poorpress.net**

## Dedication

To my folks, you know who you are, who gathered at the island park, WE OUTSIDE.

In reading this book, my hope is that we digest and know the challenge, the work, the tilling of the soil.

For I is we…

## Author's note

I am compelled and driven, more so than ever, to recapture and document this amazing work using food and the spiritual legacy of the Black Panther Party. It is an honor to tell the original herstory of Self Help Hunger Program as the Visionary. This book is my gift of struggle to the movement.

This book is written from my own words and defies linguistic domination, as a person with academic trauma from the man's school. For more on linguistic domination, see *Poverty Scholarship: Poor People-Led Theory, Art, Words & Tears Across Mama Earth* at www.poorpress.net

# Credits

This book and Self Help Hunger Program would not have been possible without the real life exchange of acquaintances that I have valued over time.

**Food Justice Organizations:** Berkeley Food Network, Food Not Bombs, Sweet Adeline, South Berkeley Community Church, Phat Beets, St. Paul AME Church, Philips Temple, McGee Baptist Church, Mama's Kitchen (Amma), Manna from Heaven

**My Family:** Carl Moore, Jackie Moore, Lorenzo (Eugene) Moore, *Bernice Moore, Brittany Moore, Carla Moore, Bria Moore, Nikia Moore, Carl Moore Jr., Bianca Moore, *Debra Ambrose, Shaka Garland

**My Grandchildren:** *Aselah Pacheco, Amean, Amina, Dominique Jr., Dominique Twice, Pilar Harley

**My God Children:** Marsean, Kody (K.O.)

**SHHP Pioneers:** *Princess Beverly Williams, *Max Cadji, *Josh Cadji, *Darvel Parks, Greg Hewett, *Larry Quan

**Solidarity Support:** *Osha Newman, *Dr. Omowale Fowles, *Diane Golden

Sofia Tudose, Rachel Godfred, Beverley Wons, Sandra Franklin, Debra Cooper, Keith Gholson, Miss Pinky, Shaka Cry Baby Shay. MG BOYZ, Cedric, Calvin, Isha & Rhonda, Ebony, Sharonda Hill. Byron Vincent, Jennifer Phillips, Rodney Phillips, Jackie Phillips, Courtney, Antoine, Lisa "Tiny" Gray-Garcia, Momii Palapaz, Chester, *Rashan Bingham (life partner), People's Park, Jocelyn & Michelle (helpers in the beginning). Jessie Squire, Ann Olivia, NORJC, Selah, Alexis, Daryl, Christopher, Tony, and Ayanna. Isky Chishty, Franco Balducci (friend of 26 years), Gayle Dickson, Melvin Dickson, Paula Page, Bernadine Evans, Annie Jones, Michelle Cortez, Kamaya Robinson, Mike Green, Nate Williams, Kedar Akbar, Tina Dotson, Annie Jones, Tyrone Gupton, Ron Smith, Carl Goss, Rick da Rula, Stephanie Posey, Da Posey family, Aaron Robinson, Celeste Thomas, Crystal Drake & children, Joe Mayiah-Farley, Tony Thomas, Arlene Edwards, Varali family, Linda (50) Jackson, Ray Jackson, Pierre, HD, Netta Morris, Charles Simon, Marion Siddie, Amina Pittman, Ernest Pittman. Graphics: Corine Richardson, Dan Nguyen, Anika Karwicz, Jennifer Phillips, Sonny Philips, Rodney Phillips, Mr. Cooper, Gary Gasaway, Janice Sampson, Tina Dotson George, Bernice Moore*, Jeremiah Robinson, Cheyenne Robinson. K.B. Country, Malcolm, A1, Francine, Carl, Ms. Loretta, Lynell, B.C., Ms. Dorothy, Shirley Boddie, Gary Gasaway, Mama Janice, Sue Marks, Tyrone Gupton, Rufus Gupton, Stanford Market, Tony, DeMarcus, Ron Smith, Maya Ram, Tiny, A.S. Ikeda. The Defend Aunti Francis Coalition: Felix, Ariel, Eleanor & many others. APTP: cuz yall are the power of the people - Ase. The BPP Collective Comrades, DeeColonize Academy, POOR Magazine and POOR Press.

So many people have come and gone over the years of Self Help Hunger Program. I know there's many more people that I didn't name. To list them would not be easy, but I appreciate your time and work of love. Thank you for everything you have done to help this movement sprout and be!

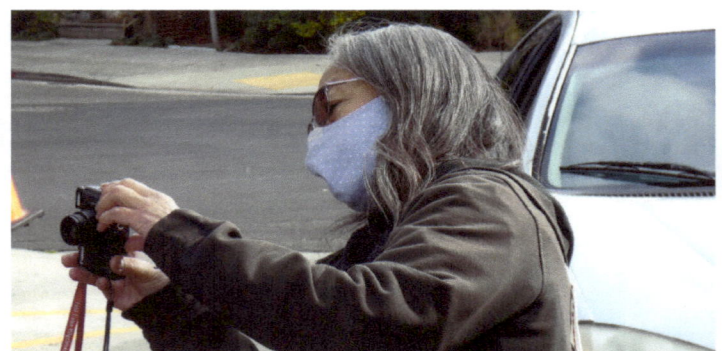

## Table of Contents

**Chapter 1.** The Kitchen That Fed So Many — 7

**Chapter 2.** All Produce to the People — 12

**Chapter 3.** The Free Food Wars — 15

**Chapter 4.** GentriFUKation — 15

**Chapter 5.** Standing Our Ground — 19

**Chapter 6.** The Garden of Souls — 22

**Chapter 7.** Here and Now — 24

**Memorials** — 26

**Self Help Hunger Program Past Events** — 27

# Chapter 1
## The Kitchen That Fed So Many

Before I moved to this place, I was living in a dwelling that Franco Balducci (my friend of 24 years) had built. It was four condos on 38th and Ruby here in Oakland. It was brand new, built from the ground up with various investors, including the bank. We were staying there for one year during the completion of the other units, but time was running out. It took us too long to rent it out or sell it, so the bank snatched it from us.

So we were desperate. Where are we going to live? I had friends, and I asked my friend Michael O. if he had a place for us. And he had one. I got it as-is. That's how I moved to 811 61st Street. I didn't realize that my friend would turn out to be a slumlord, but I soon found out. It was our last "option" to move from those new condos into a substandard living space large enough to house us. We had a roof over our heads, but it was a total rat trap with no amenities whatsoever. At this place, I endured mice, mold, no heat, leaky roof…and let me stop there. We went from a jacuzzi bathroom and gourmet kitchen and all that, to this. This was so depressing to endure, such a drastic change. I was depressed for weeks after that. But like it or not, this was the beginning. This was the place that would feed many and provide many shelter from the elements.

It was in my kitchen, a very simple one with no amenities, that Self Help Hunger Program started. When I first moved in, it was practically bare, but it did have a stove, refrigerator, and sink—that was truly about all it had in the square box room called the kitchen. Little by little, I had my roommate Franco put up shelves and a new faucet.

That was in maybe the late nineties, early 2000s. I used to cook up a pot in my old place and bring it right out here, and folks would come, and I'd serve food to them. It was a perfectly good idea to use the kitchen to cook and carry the meal down the block to the park. I would ask the churches for plates and forks and things like that. And then we would take HIV tests so that we could get the gift cards. Then we would put our gift cards together to go to Safeway. Once we gathered food from using the Safeway gift cards and standing in free food lines, the meal was

set. During those times, we ate a lot of beans flavored with smoked turkey wings, cornbread of course, cheap rice we got for free, salad, fruit (thanks to Phat Beets), and dessert thanks to Sweet Adeline Bakery. During the early days, we fed about 12 people or maybe less. Over the years, we built shelving and even bought a used washer and dryer, through which I began providing laundry service for the houseless.

Moving to 61st Street was my first intro to this pocket park called Driver Plaza. Here were the people I had spent time with when I was homeless, surviving in the streets. Driver Plaza is located between South Berkeley and North Oakland. This park used to be owned by the Drivers, a Black family. It's been a social hotspot for generations and generations. I remember hearing about this place from years before, when my sister used to come hang out here. It remains the place where folks hang out, play dominoes or cards, grill, or just be hussling, trying to make a blood-stained dollar.

The first time I brought food out to Driver Plaza was 15 years ago. At that time, I was deep in struggle, dealing with depression and my mental health. I got to know the people that used to hang out in the park. It was wild, real wild. Over the years, I had worked in various soup kitchens. Especially when I was homeless. And the reason why I started working in kitchens in the first place was because I was tired of standing in line with my hand out. So my first attempt to work in those kitchens was to get out of line and say, "Hey, can I wash the pots for my meal?" So I ended up washing pots and then they asked me to volunteer. I volunteered in soup kitchens for so many years. And they said, "Well, can you cook?" I could cook. "Well, you want to be the head cook?" And that's how I started doing that. And then Gayle Dickson, who was also a Panther, started the Friday Night Art and Dinner program at the church. It was designed to get all the children in the community to come on Friday night to have dinner and work on an art project. And I was all about that. Working with Gayle was medicine, despite my struggle of homelessness. She made a great contribution to the infamous neighborhood of South Berkeley and to the children who she served, using food to unify the neighborhood and implementing art while providing nutritious food for the children. I volunteered there and started cooking for this program.

Mind you, I was still struggling that whole time. And I was using that outlet to fill some of my time—I was putting something back in. So that was my little outlet. It was like medicine. It was a pause from the pain. But mind you, once I left that soup kitchen, it was hard. But here I was, just moved to 61st street. The people that were in this little park were the ones I used to hang out with. So we said, "Hey, we're hungry now because we done drank all day, and Top Ramen ain't gonna do it." So it got me thinking, because I was working in those kitchens and I was realizing how important it is for folks who have challenges—the substance abuse, the alcoholism, the mental health challenges—to have access to food. We need food.

Well, I had the kitchen. I said, "Hey, I got the kitchen because I live right there." So I thought, let's pool all our money and resources, and then I'll go up there and cook, and then I'll bring the pot down. And that's how it started.

Most times, I would cook in my kitchen and then we would also barbecue out in the park. There was a barbecue pit out in the park. And I call this land of this pocket park the titty. It's a titty because so many people can get nutrition

and get nourished off of this land—and that's just what a titty is. And so there was about 6 people who lived out here in Driver Plaza. And the park provided those things that they needed. It provided food, it provided shelter, it provided community. This was the spot, and it still is.

I figured if we can piece up on alcohol, we can piece up on food. One thing led to another, and after I did it for a while, somebody else said, "Hey, can I help?" He lived right behind me. I said, "Sure." After we started growing a little bit bigger, I started using my SSI money to go to the dollar store. We were totally fucking over Mama Earth, because I was getting their styrofoam plates since they were the cheapest. And you could get canned goods there as well. But this was out of my pocket. And we started getting bigger and people started to show up and expect us to be there with the food. People started to look forward to a hot, home-cooked meal. We insisted on keeping it balanced, and served food at least once a week. But the food was just one thing. It wasn't just all I had to do.

I started thinking: why did this place look like a dumping site? There was a mess. Where a tree stands now, it used to be blanketed with beer bottles and all types of debris. After I put my food on in the kitchen, I started to come down and sweep. I would tell people off. I would say, "Put your trash in the proper receptacle." This would later become a familiar phrase at the island park.

Because I've been organizing for so many years, this is about more than just trash. I would preach, cuss, and fuss. You must keep your eyes open when you are surrounded by gentrification.

At any moment, the City can come and fence this place off. In the face of that, we have to show that we're organized and that we're good stewards of the land. That means we need order, cleanliness, and structure. That is people power. The City of Oakland don't come and do the grass or anything—we do that. Even to this day. We clean the bathrooms. Occasionally, the City comes in to provide services. But we do all the daily maintenance. We must do it because the City threatened us like we were a nuisance, even though most of us live or used to live here. They wanted us to disappear. They never provided accommodations like water, toilets, or garbage removal. I look at it like a choke-out, like a war—denying us our basic needs or any provisions that would enhance our existence in this tiny park. By staying organized, we have stayed in this park, and we have definitely grown since we first started out.

I learned to organize the community from being a Black Panther. People power and structure and being good stewards of the land and making sure that the gentrifiers don't come and fence you off—that's all the legacy of the Panther Party. That's how you keep on doing good work. And when you do good work, the people start supporting you and lifting you up.

When we first got here, it was just me alone with a drive to provide food and cleanliness, even outside in a park. Over time, the food came in and that component started growing. We rolled our shopping carts to the park and we got our three-course meal—we got the salad, and we got the dessert. That's what self-help is—it means making sure that everybody in the community puts in. We saw Sweet Adeline, the bakery down the street, and said, "Hey, we need your desserts." And this neighbor said they were going to give us $30 a month. We can use that. We can ask, "Hey, do you have any seasoning over here?" or, "Who got some rice?" and someone answers, "Oh, I got some." This is the heart and soul of self-help. Everybody puts in, and everybody gets fed. We don't feed the few, we feed the multitude.

*Original Brochure, designed by Larry Quan.*

"Picnic on de Island"
Tuesdays @ 2 PM

. . .

Come Join Us
@ Triangle Park
where Adeline meets
Stanford

. . .

"We don't just feed
the Homeless,
We feed the Hungry"

Darvel Parks

## Helpful Resources

**Aunti Frances Love Mission**
(510) 395-5988

### FOOD
Aunti Frances Food Program
Berkeley Food Pantry
Food Not Bombs Peoples Park
Trinity Breakfast
St. Paul African Methodist

### Clothing
Berkeley Drop-In Center
Salvation Army
Good Will

### Shelter
VA Emergency Shelter
Berkeley Drop-In Center
(ask for Shelter Plus Care
& Tenant Support Program)

## Aunti Frances Love Mission

(510) 395-5988

### Self Help Hunger Program

Frances Moore, Director

## MISSION STATEMENT

We represent a collective of folks who live in the South Berkeley neighborhood & community. Some of us are without homes or shelter; some of us were born and raised in the area ~ but ALL OF US are simply drawn together BONDING WITH EACH OTHER Regardless of our present state or economic status, WE COME TOGETHER (not always easy - but we do it) ! We believe that the positive energy, the drive and the divine inspiration lead us to pull together as a unified community of *SELF-HELP* (each one help one) Thus, we endeavor to provide HELP & SERVICES to Individuals & Families not merely to help them Survive but to help them THRIVE !

*Get Involved Now*

## You Can Help Make a Difference

with your Generous Donations

. . .

Bring new Hope to those in Need

. . .

Get a Bright Smile from those who appreciate because they know YOU CARE

## SHINING STARS
### Participants & Contributors

| | |
|---|---|
| Michelle Jackson | Joselyn Gholsom |
| Pinky Thomas | Keith Gholsom |
| Vernon Andrews | Sandra Franklin |
| Greg Williams | John (Poncho) Ellis |
| Lorenzo Quan | Ed Williams |
| Chester Watts | Jerome Hatcher |
| Rufus Gupton | Tyrone Gupton |
| Emmitt Hutson | Joe Stephens |
| Darnell Butcher | Phillip Butcher |
| Loretta Jones | Carl Gross |
| Greg Hewitt | Loretta Jones |
| Leon Cooper Jr. | Earl Davis |
| Adrian Bates | Mark Ward |
| Garland Albert | Trevor Jackson |
| Barbara Sloan | Willie Reed |
| Daoud Dockery | Robert Humhprey |
| Eddie Cooper | Kedar Ellis Akbar |
| Chris H. | Manna From Heaven |
| Downs Memorial | J & B Market |
| Berkeley Drop-In | St Paul AME Church |
| Stanford Market | Phillips Temple |
| Creative Energy Resource Center | |

This is the original mission statement of Self Help Hunger Program: "We represent a collective of folks who live in the South Berkeley/North Oakland neighborhood and community. Some of us are without homes or shelter; some of us were born and raised in the area — but ALL OF US are simply drawn together BONDING WITH EACH OTHER. Regardless of our present state or economic status, WE COME TOGETHER (not always easy — but we do it)! We believe that the positive energy, the drive and a divine inspiration lead us to pull together as a unified community of SELF-HELP (each one help one). Thus, we endeavor to provide HELP & SERVICES to individuals and families not merely to help them survive but to help them THRIVE!"

Larry Quan is very important to Self Help Hunger Program. He was the one who did the flier, our original brochure. He was helping me in the beginning, and he had graphic design skills. He would also come and make Chinese food for the people, like shrimp fried rice. We would sit and talk about things and I said, "We need a brochure." He said, "Yeah, I can help you with that." He helped me with my first poster. It was beautiful and helped us reach the community. I'm very grateful. Larry Quan is very, very important.

# Chapter 2
## All Produce to the People

To talk about the produce stand, I really need to mention Max Cadji and Phat Beets. Both were very, very inspirational and gave me a lot of assistance, guidance, love, support, and direction. He encouraged me to speak up and out for the people we serve. Max Cadji was the visionary of Phat Beets Produce. And he's the one who introduced me to the concept of food justice and ways to provide proper nutritional food to the community. As you know, in the beginning, I was buying dollar-store styrofoam plates and cups, canned this and pre-prepared that. My experience with Phat Beets taught me how to feed the people proper food.

I met Max during a time when we were having an altercation with gentrifiers in the new development. I remember the town hall meeting. Gentrifiers were complaining about the pocket park and the people and the loud talking and the loud music and all that. Max heard about the town hall, and he came and did some mediation. He caught wind of our battle and intervened through North Oakland Restorative Justice Council. We also did a peace walk, which was the start of the friendship between Max and me.

Then, Max contacted a friend of his named Phoenix. Phoenix was the assistant of Dan Kalb, our City Councilmember. Well, she was pro-people and was very proactive. She came in and attempted to mediate, to see what the City of Oakland could do to better help us and serve us. She helped replace the benches, and she also donated turkey and all the trimmings for our ThanksTaking (Thanksgiving) meal. We built a close relationship, despite the fact that Dan Kalb is Dan Kalb.

In this mediation process, Santa Fe CAN (Community Association & Neighbors), a group of people in the Santa Fe neighborhood here in North Oakland, came forth and adopted the park. They were interested in what we were doing because we were in their/our neighborhood. And we formed work parties. Dan Kalb only came here because the wealthy people in the neighborhood were complaining. "Who are these people?" "Why are they here?" "Why are they feeding people?" So Dan Kalb came up physically and set up a meeting with a few of us, Santa Fe CAN, and the police, to see what was going on. Well, Santa Fe CAN decided to do work parties with the "Have More" and the "Have Less." And when we had food, unfortunately we were also cleaning up needles and alcohol bottles. So we started doing it on our own. Dan Kalb stood right here and said he didn't believe that we could work together. But he made a promise that if we could work together, he would assist us in the various things we needed. After our table discussion between Sante Fe CAN, the police, and ourselves, I talked to Nate Williams

of Santa Fe CAN, who is still with us and helps us with the garden. We looked at each other and said, "It's going to take a lot of work." Over the years, Santa Fe CAN kind of faded out. But we're still here doing the work.

And it's really funny, when you start doing this type of work, people start paying attention. And then organizations that are doing similar things, they start getting connected. Our presence and food attracted attention, especially because we were doing something positive.

As a matter of fact, the produce stand started out with just two crates. And look at it now. At that time, Phat Beets would give away free produce in front of the doctor's office down the street. In the early days I would go to them and pick out stuff to bring here. And over time, as we got to talking, Max started to give me any remaining produce that they had left over. Phat Beets was operating CSA boxes once a week. So with that, I could come and get produce to fill the two crates as well. Phat Beets even gave me a garden plot in Dover Park so I could start planting and growing food myself. My first garden project was growing potatoes.

Later, we also connected up with Food Not Bombs. I would go to Food Not Bombs when they had their produce and I could get surplus from them too. So that's how that started. So people at Self Help Hunger Program would get produce. Once we had more than just a few crates, Susan Quinlan actually built one of the parts of the produce stand out of wood. And then thanks to Max Cadji, some high school students from Castlemont did the etchings on the produce stand.

Once we made connections, we were able to then hook up with organizations like Berkeley Food Network, Manna from Heaven, ECAP, and get more produce. And as we got more produce, we created a larger produce stand. So we had more space and we had more produce to give out. We were able to serve more people. And now the churches who do their food program, they bring us their surplus. So the bigger the produce stand is, the more food we are able to provide for people.

I should mention, it is the Melvin Dickson Memorial Free Produce Stand: All Produce to the People. That's very important. Melvin Dickson and I served in the Black Panther Party together. Melvin was the editor of the *Commemorator* newspaper, which was run by The Commemoration Committee for the Black Panther Party. He started that paper and now he has transitioned. Melvin was always my go-to person. I was always shy and insecure about speaking. I said, "Melvin, what do I say?" He would tell me, "Just speak the truth and speak from the heart." And he would always back me up. He used to come out here and speak at events over the years. And eventually, he would come to get produce because he had cancer. Melvin did such important work for the party and for Self Help.

The vision of Self Help Hunger Program is that food can be a form of organizing community. It is very important because there are food

*Melvin Dickson Memorial Free Produce Stand: All Produce to the People*

deserts that are dying on the vine all around us. Berkeley Bowl is way up there, and their food is very high priced. It's ridiculous. Not to mention the closing of discount grocery stores, like the Grocery Outlet that was in our area or the People Community Market on San Pablo. And on top of that, the dollar stores are closing and are moving to the suburban areas. With all the stores closing around us in the nearby neighborhoods, the food desert is growing.

This produce stand is very crucial. And I'm seeing an increase of people coming to the stand. It used to be basically this social club, the people that always come. Now it's the neighbors, and it's people driving from other cities coming here. And it's amazing. So I think this is a hub for resources. It feeds so many people now, and it is just wonderful to see that we can use this land for public good. We don't know how long we're going to be here, but while we're here, let's be good stewards and let's give and love. I don't want to be so cliché, but it takes love. It takes love for me to still be here in 15 years after all the struggle, not only with the City, not only with the police, but with the people I serve. So, yeah, it's a good thing.

# Chapter 3
## The Free Food Wars

In the beginning, I would go to different food distributions to collect and stockpile food for our meal. But some places were not as welcoming. There was a little resistance from people who were operating the distribution, the handout, the food giveaway. It used to be like, "This is ours." And, "Why are you taking so much?" And I'm explaining, "Well, I have a food ministry." I would try to show them a pamphlet. "Here, this is who I am. This is why I'm taking more food." But all of this took time. There was resistance. And I just wanted to show how hard it was. It took a lot of work to get up early and stand in line. If you wanna be number one in line, that means you're getting up at five. You're going to wait until they open the doors at seven, but you're there at six. And you probably have to do this every day at a different place. Every day it's, "No, why is she taking that?" And someone had to explain, "She has a food ministry." Week after week, waking up early to stand in line and explaining over and over again—it was hard. That struggle is real.

It's not so much like that now, because we're established now. And now the people that used to be hesitant to give me food are bringing their surplus here.

I had to work through that. Consistency, longevity, all that to stay standing. I really would like this book to be a template for other communities to reach out and help each other. To generate food together, housing support together. Find another pocket park or find something to that effect and make something happen for your community. Because it is a struggle, it's always a struggle even to this day. And when it gets hard, the only thing I can do is just pray. That's the only way I was able to get through it and just think of a solution. How can I better this situation?

And it's hard. I mean, I've had fist fights out here, and I've won every fight. I feel that when right's on your side, you better watch out.

But there's times I've been scared, very scared. So I have my folks who love me surrounding me. Putting their bodies in front of danger. Other times if somebody's got a knife, I've made it to my car and I pick up my club, wanting to fight. But then I have to reserve myself because I'm Aunti Frances and that's just going to start retaliation. So I suck it up. I'll be humble. Even though I'm scared, I stand my ground. I don't know what else to do. But I believe that the work that I'm doing protects me, that emotion of giving and love. And I think that I'm protected to a certain degree.

But being in this place and doing this work in struggle for so long, I have enemies, too, now. People who are jealous of me or who judge me. But I think, "Why? Why are you jealous of this? You could be doing the same thing. I'm not doing nothing special. Not a damn thing special. You can do the same thing."

# Chapter 4
## GentriFUKation*

During the spike of gentrification, I really realized what it was all about. I was paying attention to all these tents popping up in the area. It was outrageous. At the time, I felt so grateful to be blessed with a place to stay. And then gentrification, that monster, came knocking on my door. The land that I was residing on at 61st Street was nice piece of land, and it was a lure to all the greedy Devil-opers (developers), and all the greedy slumlords, and all the greedy folks who don't give a fuck about destroying people's lives by displacing them. They came knocking on my door. I scared off at least three homeowners. One was, when you come into my house, all the memorabilia of progress and the Black Panthers. They figured they didn't want to mess with me. Then I started with my bipolar. I snapped on a couple of people because I got sick and tired of the circus of developers coming into my house and looking at stuff. When you do a home view, an open house, they're coming into your home. All hours of the day, they come looking around. And so I stopped a couple and said, "Hey, ain't no showing today. I'm not feeling it."

Then the other ones were scam developers. And they came knocking on the door like a snake, all friendly. They tried to be so slick and cunning and say, "I'm here to help you." "If you move, we will help you find better place." "This can be a blessing in disguise." And they sent out their assistant to my place, to help me look for another place. We actually became good friends, because she was a mother in struggle as well. She eventually became homeless. I saw her not too long ago. But at that time, she was working for the scam corporation, and eventually it turned around and bit her. One time she said, "Frances, I have some people that come see you." And I cried and said, "I can't do it. No, let 'em go away." People I don't even know in my house looking around, snooping. She was very compassionate. She said, "We'll come back another time."

I eventually realized that, since she had to put food on the table, she was working for the problem. And then those scam developers sold the property to someone else. It was so sneaky. They weren't even an LLC. They turned out to be even slimier than I thought. And, later, I came to find out they owned this and owned that, and they weren't as true blue as they said. And the sister, their assistant, broke it down to me. She said they sold my place to someone else. And this is the person who succeeded in getting me out of there.

He comes with his bullshit, saying he wanted to move a family member into my home. They came up with a "no-fault" eviction. Back in the day, you only got evicted if you didn't pay your rent or if you did property damage. But they found a loophole.

---

* **GentriFUKation** — word remix from the GentriFUKation Tours-R-Us theatre action by POOR Magazine / Theatre of the POOR

*2018 Stolen Land Hoarded Resources UnTour through so-called Beverly Hills*

So we fought. We fought with everything we could. We went to court, we did campaigns, we sent them letters, we went to City Council meetings, we researched. I had a bonafide support group that was bad-fucking-ass. We even made up Christmas cards. We intimidated and we harassed the owners, big time. We put a big banner outside of my house that read "Let Aunti Frances Stay! Stop gentrification!" Right in front of my house. That was intimidating. People were calling them all hours of the day, people knocking on their door. Neighbors were even saying, don't evict her. Let her stay. Even the children got involved. This group called Abundant Beginnings came and rallied all down the street. And then we had a rally that was at least 200 people. We marched in front of the house. We were fighting so hard. We went to court. I even had court support when I went to court. There was breakfast. All these people showed up to support me in court and outside of the courtroom. And when I finally did see the judge, the judge said, "Are all of those people out there for you?"

Having such strong support, we were able to close the loopholes. But I got nervous. And I got scared. I didn't trust the unjust judicial system. In the end, I broke and went for the money. It was a nice piece, but not enough. It seemed like a big amount of money, but with moving everything and with being disabled and having to hire people, I blew through a good amount of it. It was so disheartening to throw and give away some of my personal effects. Even today, I can recall those items I cherished.

But I still feel blessed about the overall outcome. It really showed me the power of the people. What's so remarkable and amazing about my eviction defense is that people came from everywhere. People I didn't even know. The core group for my defense came and cleaned my house out. They went and advocated for me to get a place. A homeowner cold-called me and said, "Hello, I hear you're looking for a place. I'm going to ask the students to move out so you can move in." This is the place I live now. She pays for my housekeeper every three weeks. She pays for all utilities. And we have a good relationship. When I had mold, she put me in an

Airbnb so she could tear up the walls and pull up the carpet. She washed my clothes.

But my eviction was heartbreaking. Totally heartbreaking. I had at least 32 people, not all at one time, that I had opened my doors to. They could stay with me, so it was a house for many. The place I have now is too small for anyone else. It's just enough space for me. I'm not doing sleepovers or extended stays anymore because of that.

I'm grateful and blessed I didn't have to sleep on anyone's couch, move in with my family, and didn't have to return to the streets. It was amazing. There's so many articles, from the *Chronicle* to the radio, all about my eviction and trying to stop it. I say that I'm blessed. To this day, I still ask, why me? At Self Help we do housing support, emphasis on support. There's no magic bullet. I hate for people to even come up to me and ask me about housing because it just breaks my heart. You really, really have to be prepared for a fight. And most people just aren't because the people power just isn't there. What happened to me was a blessing. For the first 5+

years, I had no plans—just cook, cuss, fuss, and love. It was divine empowerment for me to even keep on doing this.

Many times in this love struggle, I've wanted to quit. Over the years, I've experienced people throwing my tables, ripping down my signs, saying, "Fuck you, bitch," having fist fights, all of that. I'd be coming home at the end of the day and say, "Fuck it, I'm out." Are you kidding me? Talking about ungrateful people. And guess what? In the morning, I rise. I come back and shine. I cook with love, and cook with compassion, and cook to nourish. Not to just put something together, but to really spread love and share blessings.

At the time we were starting out, I didn't have a car. I had a moped, and in rain, sleet, or snow, I was up, standing in lines, gathering up food and supplies. I didn't have resources, but I made the meal work, and we ate. It was gratifying when people started to take part in our meals.

Darvel Parks was someone who started to help out. Darvel, out of a whole group of people, stepped up and said, "Can I help you?" He offered to cook and to bring supplies and all that. He happened to be taking care of his mom, who was in one of the senior citizens' homes right around the corner from my house. Matter of fact, I could open my back door and say, "Hey, you got some onions?" And he would say, "Yeah, I got a couple. You need some?" So it started out like that, where we would make sure we had everything we needed.

Since I was fully financing the food and supplies at the beginning, we decided we would alternate who cooks and who supplies and finances the meal. Mind you, we were only feeding maybe 25 people at the time. A lot of them were our folks who we used to sleep in campgrounds with. Darvel and I worked together for at least four years.

We would borrow tables from the senior center and the seniors began to know us. There's a picture of two women, I don't know where they are now, but they were my heart. Then we had a Romanian woman who didn't speak English much, but she knew us and she would come by, too. I don't know where she is either. I've seen so many people come and go.

Then Darvel's mother died, and then he was faced with being displaced. He was his mama's caretaker and was living with her, so, when she transitioned, he had to leave the area to find somewhere else to be. That was a major loss. There's been many, many more losses since that loss. But I must give Darvel his acknowledgement, and let him know in my writing that I appreciate his help and I wish him well. In addition, I want to thank Rachael Godfrey, AIR, and Princess Beverly.

# Chapter 5
## Standing Our Ground

The neighborhood was changing. We got a table and benches, and it was great to have more seating. But the neighbors said, "Oh, that's great, people can get to sit out there and drink." One neighbor actually brought some shit—actual shit. She wrapped it up, walked to the park and confronted a group of people, saying "This is your people's shit." Another neighbor would get up early in the morning to dig in the garbage can, carefully pulling out empty alcohol bottles and cans and lining them up neatly. They took pictures and sent them to the City. I have so many stories of just plain ignorance and cultural incompetence. They need the medicine of People Skool at POOR Magazine.

At the time I lived on 61st. One morning, the City decided to come take the table out. Somebody ran up there to my house, "Hey, they're coming to take the table!" I ran out the house with my gown on and stood on that table and said, "This is mine. Do not touch it." Just standing my ground and saying, *We are still here*. And we had to stand our ground many times. I had to even have a meeting with the Chief of Police and the beat cop and all of that.

They didn't want us to be here in general. Not to mention, then we get a Porta-Potty. And we had to stand our ground on that too. That's when POOR Magazine and Deecolonize Academy came in and supported me. We went and did an action in front of Oakland Shitty (City) Hall, standing our ground. And the youth skolaz of Deecolonize Academy, they were out there chanting in front of City Hall and made a cardboard Porta-Potty to reiterate the struggle of getting basic, human accommodations. They did a demonstration and the theme was, "Where do we pee?"

That's how I got introduced to POOR Magazine, a poor & Indigenous people–led media, education, art, and land movement. Somebody who used to come and eat here told them about us. And then I did meet Tiny at an event, but I thought she was a crazy white girl. I thought, "Oh boy, here we go again." And then she spit off those words. Powerful love and truth. So I got her number and I called. She said they were starting a school. And the more I got involved with POOR Magazine, the stronger I felt. It's just healing. And it was like being in the Black Panther Party, with the camaraderie I miss and love. I had some knocks along the way, but my involvement is now on a different level. So it's like I found my party. I found them. They're here. From the Black Panther Party to POOR Magazine.

A REVOLUTIONARY NEWSPAPER 4 THA' BLACKARTHUR NEIGHBORHOOD

# Decolonewz

DECOLONIZE ACADEMY/HOMEFULNESS PRESENTS:

# Aunti Frances and the Self Help Hunger Program

## Driver Plaza is full of survivors.
BY ASELAH

Like when u can't enjoy a cold beer without having the police say "boy, put that beer in the trash or I'll do it for you and it won't be pretty" and verbal abuse and that's not the most of it they circle around the plaza and give mean looks. Drivers Plaza is a small pocket park located in South Berkeley on 61st & Martin Luther King Jr Way.

The self-help Hunger program is at Driver Plaza and is a food program to anyone who want or needs food. Aunti Frances, my grandmother, a revolutionary Black Panther and member of the POOR Magazine family, is the person who founded it and started this from the beginning.

The process is very big: we have to go shopping every Monday and cook over night sometimes and we also always serve salad.

## The Legacy of the Black Panther Party
By Tiburcio

"I'm carrying on the legacy of the Black Panther Free Food Program," said Francis Moore, the founder of the Auntie Frances Self Help Hunger Program. I was interviewing her in Driver Plaza, a small stretch of land between Genoa Street, 61st and Stanford Ave in North Oakland.

My friends and I at Deecolonize Academy went over to Driver Plaza to interview Francis about an incident that occurred last weekend. What happened was the middle to upper-class gentrifier neighbors pulled up many of the plants that she planted on the land overnight.

She is sure that the reason that they did that is because they do not want her to support the original community the black and brown people who have lived in that area longer than the gentrifiers. "This is the city of Oakland attacking us they don't want us to be here," she said with a depressed sigh.

When I asked other people what they thought of the Self Help Hunger Program Leroy Moore a disability scholar and revolutionary journalist with POOR magazine said "Its the real thing"

Aselah Pacheco, granddaughter of Auntie Frances and my classmate and friend, said "Its a good thing for the community"

My opinion is that the community needs people like Auntie Frances to lift them up and support them in a community that they grew up in and love.

**Newspaper articles from *Decolonews: A Revolutionary Newspaper 4 tha BlackArthur Neighborhood*, written by DeeColonize Academy students**

### DRIVER PLAZA IS FULL OF SURVIVORS
by Aselah

Like when u can't enjoy a cold beer without having the police say "Boy, put that beer in the trash or I'll do it for you and it won't be pretty" and verbal abuse that's not the most of it they circle around the plaza and give mean looks. Driver Plaza is a small pocket park located in South Berkeley on 61st and Martin Luther King Jr. Way.

The Self Help Hunger Program is at Driver Plaza and is a food program for anyone who wants or needs food. Aunti Frances, my grandmother, a revolutionary Black Panther and member of the POOR Magazine family, is the person who founded it and started this program from the beginning.

The process is very big: we have to go shopping every Monday and cook overnight sometimes and we also always serve salad.

### THE LEGACY OF THE BLACK PANTHER PARTY

by Tiburcio

"I'm carrying on the legacy of the Black Panther Free Food Program," said Frances Moore, the founder of the Aunti Frances Self Help Hunger Program. I was interviewing her in Driver Plaza, a small stretch of land between Genoa St, 61st St and Stanford Ave in North Oakland.

My friends and I at DeeColonize Academy went over to Driver Plaza to interview Frances about an incident that occurred last weekend. What happened was the middle to upper-class gentrifier neighbors pulled up many of the plants that she planted on the land overnight.

She is sure that the reason that they did that is because they do not want her to support the original community, the Black and brown people who have lived in that area longer than the gentrifiers. "This is the City of Oakland attacking us. They don't want us to be here," she said with a depressed sigh.

When I asked other people what they thought of the Self Help Hunger Program, Leroy Moore, a disability scholar and revolutionary journalist with POOR Magazine said, "It's the real thing."

Aselah Pacheco, granddaughter of Aunti Frances and my classmate and friend, said, "It's a good thing for the community."

My opinion is that the community needs people like Aunti Frances to lift them up and support them in a community that they grew up in and love.

# Chapter 6
## The Garden of Souls

Self Help Hunger Program has our own garden now called the Garden of Souls. We do have work days, and it's all volunteers who run it. When we get the time we schedule a work party. Once again, Max was very helpful in that. He helps with the irrigation and troubleshooting any problems. And Arlene Edwards came to us, and she's a master gardener and started planning it out.

The garden started by Max planting a tree for Isaac, who got shot right here at the bus stop. He said, "Hey, let's plant a tree in his honor." So it started. And then it grew from there, from planting that tree. We planted other trees over the years. And Princess Beverly is our newest resident, my dear friend.

When a person that comes to this social spot transitions, we plant a tree in their honor, giving life to death. My nephew's in there as well. And it's so funny, on my 60th birthday, I had a gathering here. It was big. It felt so good. Anyway, they planted a tree. They planted a tree for me. And it never lived. It died. You know what I say? Because I'm alive. And only the ones who have transitioned are in the garden growing. We try to keep it as a sacred place, a peaceful place. And it has gotten pretty big. Thanks to Max Cadji and Arlene Edwards.

I actually have a picture of all of us at the beginning. We always take group shots and maybe there might've been 20 people in that picture. At least nine of them are dead. And I've seen them picked off one by one from whatever—the lack of food, the drugs, the alcohol, the mental illness, the homelessness, the depression, the desperation. The struggle is real, and it keeps on going.

At the time that this movement began, I was having mental health issues and challenges. I was in struggle and I was dealing with depression. It was very hard sometimes to get up in the morning and prepare the meal. But I did it. That's why I say it was divine intervention. Sometimes I would be so low I couldn't get up. But I thought about the people. I thought about my commitment. And that was stronger than what I was going through. Seriously. I remember those times.

You know what else, that hurts me to my heart? After the Panthers—it's like I lost a very, very close dear one to me. I miss the Panthers. I miss it. I miss the camaraderie. I miss working together. You know what I'm saying? And for a cause that we believed in a different way than we do now. And it was like a family. I don't have that here. It's

*Isaac's tree*

*Princess Beverly's flowers*

different. It's like I was in training all those years, and now I set out to do the work that I learned to do. But it's lonely. I feel lonely many, many times. But the crazy thing about it is I feel loved here.

I am the people I serve. That's why I can hang out and be here, because I took the time to bond. Most of the people I started out with are dead now. Over the years, the faces change. As people die, then the new ones come. That's how it is.

With all the loss and change, I'm starting to rely more on my comrades to help keep Self Help thriving. One of those people is Momii Palapaz. Momii has become my biggest ally. In the years to come of Self Help, we will be working side by side. In the beginning, when she first came to Self Help, she was a silent soldier and supported me in the distance. But as years go on, Momii is right there with me in the trenches. She's there all the way. When I was sick, Momii was there at the door. We're two grouchy old women together. But she gets stuff done, whatever it is, she does it. She'll be there before I can even get there. You need somebody like that, especially when things get hard. And I'm grateful to have Momii by my side at Self Help.

*Aunti Frances's nephew, Emmanuel E. Terry.*

# Chapter 7
## Here and Now

Now we're at another phase. Now we're at a phase where we are able to get funding, and funding actually comes in. Whereas in the past, I was doing everything from cooking to serving to cleaning, now we have some staff. We know it's important to keep the park clean and organized, but right across the street there's a turn-up spot. I like to drink myself—it's not what you do, but how you do it. These gentrifiers got their wine bottles, and they allowed to do that. Why do we have to be under the radar and have to put our bottles away? That's how it is in the trenches. They've taken so much of our places away already. It's imperative that we hold down this piece of land. It's very important. All around the park used to live Black families. The people that come here, their mothers and grandparents had houses all around here. These places look new, but this used to be a Black community. There used to be a consignment shop. Now, everyone who lives here has race or class privilege.

At the same time, we do have some allies living around here. It didn't happen overnight. It did not happen overnight. But if gentrifiers are going to be here, it's important that they understand the impact of their presence, and it's important that they give back and help. And it's also important that we are respectable and are good stewards of this land.

We still have some haters down here though. Before we had a bathroom down here, this woman came to us all angry. She said, "Whose shit is this?" Somebody had shit on her stairs. Well, what do you expect? We can't get a Porta-Potty. After that we actually got the Porta-Potty. I opened my window and I saw a Porta-Potty come in—it was amazing. When we built the shed in Driver Plaza, people complained about it. "They're building tiny homes," they said. Lord forbid that if it was cold and rainy, that somebody had shelter. Shame on us, right? So the City came out, and I don't know what they were doing. To this day, I still don't know. But we were prepared—that's why we put our shed on stilts, so we can move it if we need to.

Well that was the beginning. That was the gentrification. And here we are now. Self Help Hunger Program is maintaining because of the crumbs that we're allowed to pay people, which is from the money that's been coming in a little bit. We're in a very different time from the Black Panthers consciousness. We used to work our asses off 16, 17 hours a day, for no money, but for the cause. Today, we don't have that here at all. The fact is that people are struggling, so what can you say? But I can't help but miss that camaraderie that I grew up with in the Panthers. But I understand that these are different times.

Now I'm doing my outreach. I was taught revolutionary education in the Black Panther Party as a young person in the '70s. Now I've graduated, and I have to go out there and show what I know. I came up in the Party, and I was prepared for this revolutionary love work. After my time there, my wings were clipped. Now I go out there and spread it. And that's the lasting legacy of the Panthers. For 15 years in a very changing and shifting part of Oakland, me and my people have been here, struggling and surviving to build unity and self-determination among our people. This is the Self Help Hunger Program.

"Using public land, Self Help Hunger Program has been offering free food, free clothing, and free access to services for over 14 years. Based on free labor, dedication, and endless love for humankind, Self Help Hunger Program stands as a testimony to the fact that when communities are left to care for themselves, they can truly thrive."

# Memorials
## We honor the souls we have lost along the way.

Keith Gholsom
Edward Wons
Hootie Garland
Jamal Byrd
Piere
Will
Cecil
Ce Ce
Sandra Franklin
John Ellis Jr. (Poncho)
Ray Jones (Mooka)
Isaac
Big Rob
Dena
Tanala
BP
Donnie
JT
Debra Cooper
Baby James
Sheba the dog
Peanut the dog
Pansy the dog
Kathryn Davis
Hugo Thomas Anthony
Bam Bam
Jafona
Tulu
Princess Beverly
Melvin Dickson

and many others who were part of Driver Plaza and Self Help Hunger Program over the years.

# Self Help Hunger Program Past Events

# Aunti Frances' 60th Birthday Celebration

Our friend and community member, Aunti Frances Moore -- better known by some as "Aunti Frances" -- will be turning 60 years old in July! Join us in celebrating the joy that Aunti Frances brings to so much of the community. It will also highlight the Self-Help Hunger Program's grassroots food justice work done in the spirit of the Black Panther Free Breakfast Program and the legacy of self-determination it helped give root to in Oakland on Ohlone land.

There will be food, music, spoken word and groove, so come by, bring a dish and meet your neighbors and the vessels of love that continue to feed the people with so few resources yet so much passion.

**Date:** Sunday, July 19th

**Time:** 1pm

**Where:** Driver Plaza in North Oakland (Adeline and 61st St)

**RSVP**
Please RSVP to the facebook page at http://on.fb.me/1IGommR if you can make it! Share it too!

**ACCESSIBILITY**
Driver Plaza is wheelchair accessible and in an open space/park that may have chemical scents. Please email us if you have concerns about this.

**Support the event financially**
To make an in-kind donation (food, supplies, etc.) please email info@phatbeetsproduce.org. To support Aunti Frances Self-Help Hunger Program financially, please go to http://www.phatbeetsproduce.org/get-involved/donate/ and scroll down for Aunti Frances's account.

**Sponsored by:** Phat Beets Produce, POOR, Planting Justice and Farms to Grow

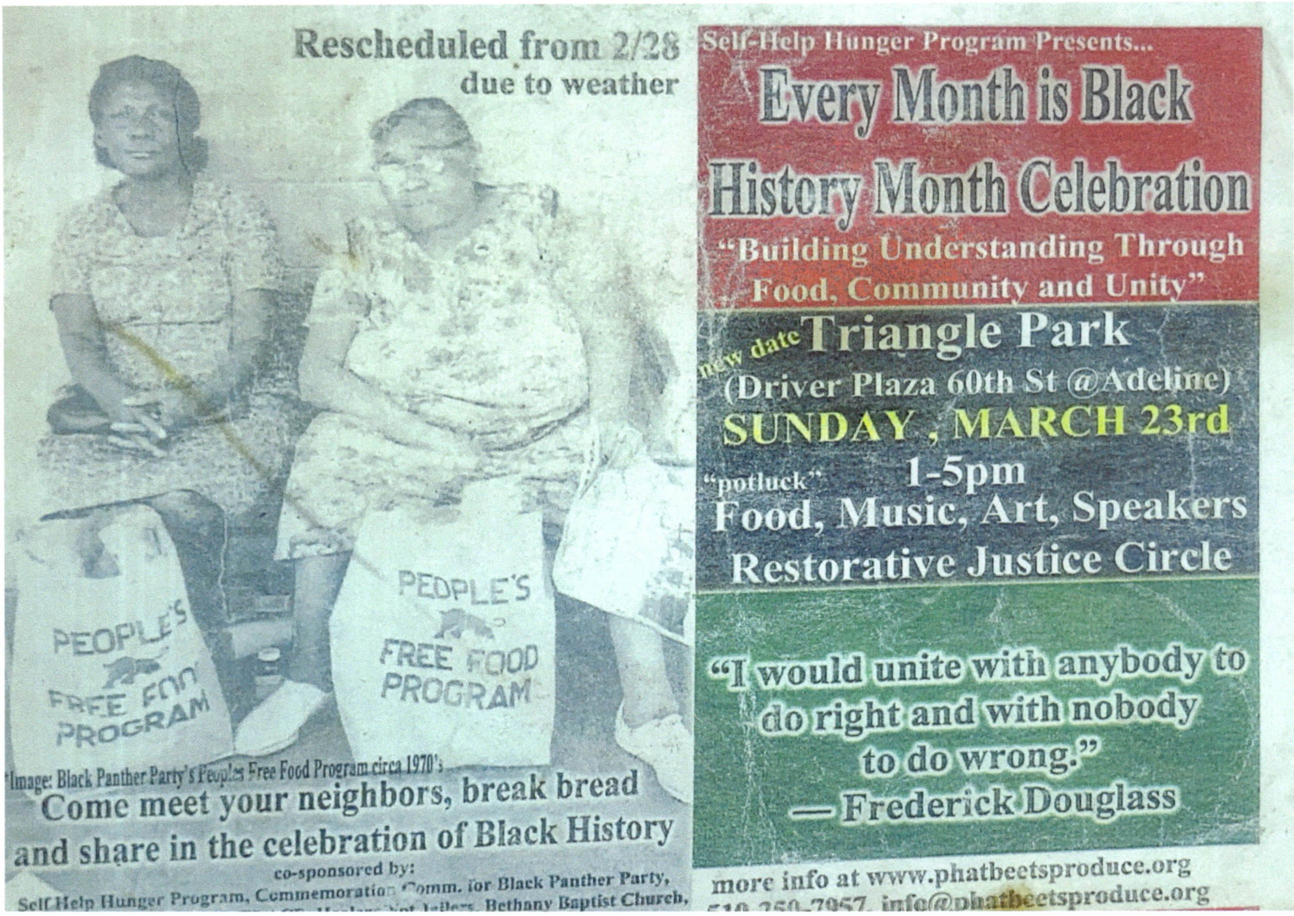
Rescheduled from 2/28
due to weather
Self-Help Hunger Program Presents...
Every Month is Black
History Month Celebration
"Building Understanding Through
Food, Community and Unity"
new date Triangle Park
(Driver Plaza 60th St @Adeline)
SUNDAY, MARCH 23rd
"potluck" 1-5pm
Food, Music, Art, Speakers
Restorative Justice Circle
PEOPLE'S
FREE FOOD
PROGRAM
"I would unite with anybody to
do right and with nobody
to do wrong."
— Frederick Douglass
*Image: Black Panther Party's Peoples Free Food Program circa 1970's
Come meet your neighbors, break bread
and share in the celebration of Black History
co-sponsored by:
more info at www.phatbeetsproduce.org

EVERY MONTH IS BLACK HISTORY
3rd Annual MONTH CELEBRATION
Fighting for Black Futures in the Ohlone Bay Area
Juneteenth Celebration by Self Help Hunger Program
North Oakland and South Berkeley
SELF HELP
HUNGER
*Music* Potluck BBQ*Circle*Speakers*Youth*
auntifrances@yahoo.com, FB: Self Help Hunger Program
Drivers Plaza "The Island"
61st and Adeline St. North Oakland
Sunday June 12th 12-6pm

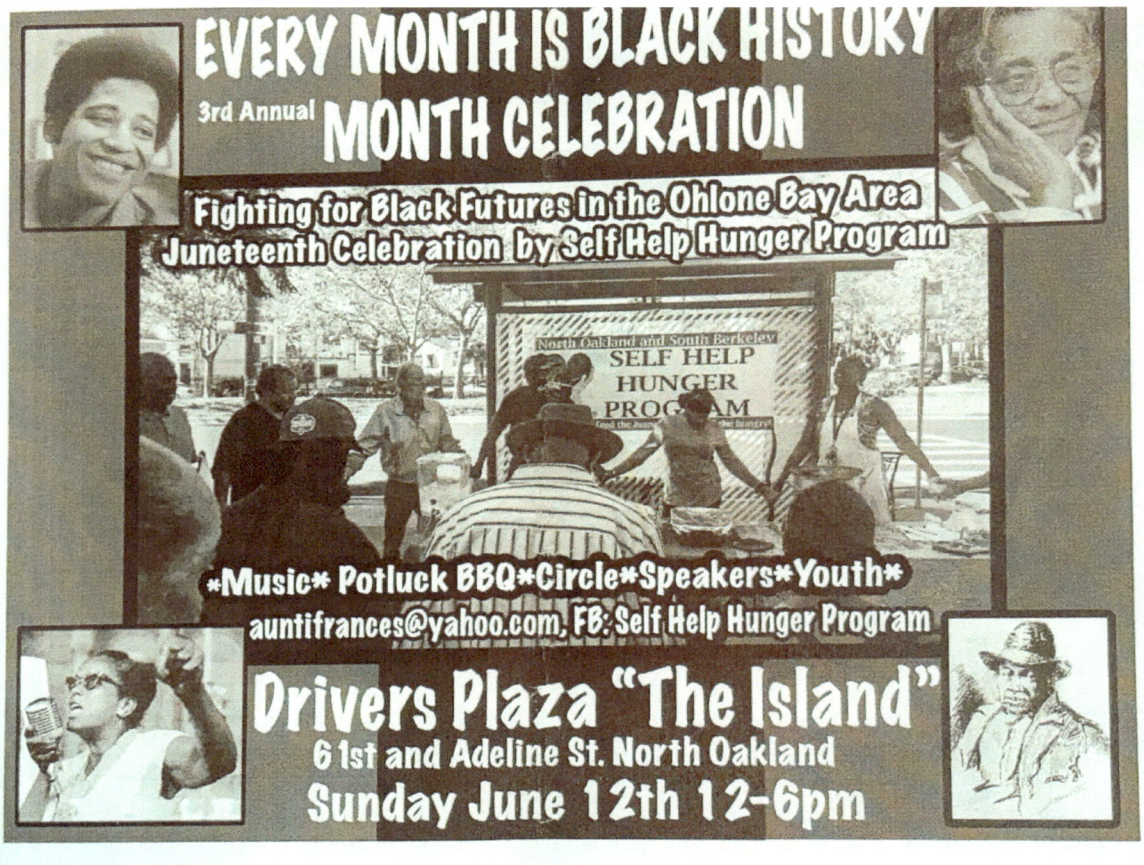